Peter Grimes

SADLER'S WELLS OPERA BOOKS

★ All royalties from the sale of these books will be employed by THE GOVERNORS to supplement a special fund for commissioning NEW operatic works in English.

Benjamin Britten.

EDITED BY ERIC CROZIER

SADLER'S WELLS OPERA BOOKS, NO. 3

BENJAMIN BRITTEN

Peter Grimes

essays by

BENJAMIN BRITTEN

E. M. FORSTER

MONTAGU SLATER

EDWARD SACKVILLE-WEST

designs by

KENNETH GREEN

published for

THE GOVERNORS OF SADLER'S WELLS FOUNDATION

BY JOHN LANE THE BODLEY HEAD

London 1946

First Published 1945
Reprinted 1946

Printed in Great Britain by
MORRISON AND GIBB LTD., LONDON AND EDINBURGH
for JOHN LANE THE BODLEY HEAD LIMITED
8 BURY PLACE, LONDON, W.C.1

CONTENTS

5

ILLUSTRATIONS

BY BENJAMIN BRITTEN

Introduction

DURING the summer of 1941, while working in California, I came across a copy of *The Listener* containing an article about George Crabbe by E. M. Forster. I did not know any of the poems of Crabbe at that time, but reading about him gave me such a feeling of nostalgia for Suffolk, where I had always lived, that I searched for a copy of his works, and made a beginning with "The Borough." Mr. Forster's article is reproduced in this book : it is easy to see how his excellent account of this "entirely English poet" evoked a longing for the realities of that grim and exciting seacoast around Aldeburgh.

Earlier in the year, I had written the music of *Paul Bunyan*, an operetta to a text by W. H. Auden, which was performed for a week at Columbia University, New York. The critics damned it unmercifully, but the public seemed to find something enjoyable in the performances. Despite the criticisms, I wanted to write more works for the stage. "The Borough"—and particularly the story of "Peter Grimes"—provided a subject and a background from which Peter Pears and I began trying to construct the scenario of an opera.

A few months later I was waiting on the East Coast for a passage back to England, when a performance of my *Sinfonia da Requiem* was given in Boston under Serge Koussevitsky. He asked why I had not written an opera. I explained that the construction of a scenario, discussions with a librettist, planning the musical architecture, composing preliminary sketches, and writing nearly a thousand pages of orchestral score, demanded a freedom from other work which was an economic impossibility for most young composers. Koussevitsky was interested in my project for an opera based on Crabbe, although I did not expect to have the opportunity of writing it for several years. Some weeks later we met again, when he told me that he had arranged for the commissioning of the opera, which was to be dedicated to the memory of his wife, who had recently died.

On arrival in this country in April 1942 I outlined the rough plan to Montagu Slater, and asked him to undertake the libretto. Discussions, revisions, and corrections took nearly eighteen months. In January 1944 I began composing the music, and the score was completed in February 1945.

For most of my life I have lived closely in touch with the sea. My parent's house in Lowestoft directly faced the sea, and my life as a child was coloured by the fierce storms that sometimes drove ships on to our coast and ate away whole stretches of the neighbouring cliffs. In writing *Peter Grimes*, I wanted to express my awareness of the perpetual struggle of men and women whose livelihood depends on the sea—difficult though it is to treat such a universal subject in theatrical form.

I am especially interested in the general architectural and formal problems of opera, and decided to reject the Wagnerian theory of "permanent melody." for the classical practice of separate numbers that crystallize and hold the emotion of a dramatic situation at chosen moments. One of my chief aims is to try and restore to the musical setting of the English language a brilliance, freedom, and vitality that have been curiously rare since the death of Purcell. In the past hundred years, English writing for the voice has been dominated by strict subservience to logical speech-rhythms, despite the fact that accentuation according to sense often contradicts the accentuation demanded by emotional content. Good recitative should transform the natural intonations and rhythms of everyday speech into memorable musical phrases (as with Purcell), but in more stylized music, the composer should not deliberately avoid unnatural stresses if the prosody of the poem and the emotional situation demand them, nor be afraid of a high-handed treatment of words, which may need prolongation far beyond their common speech-length, or a speed of delivery that would be impossible in conversation.

The scarcity of modern British operas is due to the limited opportunities that are offered for their performance. Theatre managers will not present original works without a reasonable hope of recovering their costs of production : composers and writers cannot thrive without the experience of seeing their operas adequately staged and sung : the conservatism of audiences hinders experimental departures from the accepted repertory.

In my own case, the existence of Sadler's Wells has been an incentive to complete *Peter Grimes* : the qualities of the Opera Company have considerably influenced both the shape and the characterization of the opera. Whatever its reception may be, it is to be hoped that the willingness of the Company to undertake the presentation of new operas will encourage other composers to write works in what is, in my opinion, the most exciting of musical forms.

George Crabbe : The Poet and the Man

TO think of Crabbe is to think of England. He never left our shores and he only once ventured to cross the border into Scotland. He did not even go to London much, but lived in villages and small country towns. He was a clergyman of the English Church. His Christian name was that of our national saint. Moreover, his father was also called George, and so was his grandfather, and he christened his eldest son George, and his grandson was called George also. Five generations of George Crabbes !

Our particular George Crabbe was born (in the year 1755) at Aldeborough, on the coast of Suffolk. It is a bleak little place ; not beautiful. It huddles round a flint-towered church and sprawls down to the North Sea—and what a wallop the sea makes as it pounds at the shingle ! Near by is a quay, at the side of an estuary, and here the scenery becomes melancholy and flat ; expanses of mud, saltish commons, the marsh-birds crying. Crabbe heard that sound and saw that melancholy, and they got into his verse. He worked as an unhappy little boy on the quay, rolling barrels about and storing them in a warehouse, under orders from his father. He hated it. His mother had died : his father was cross. Now and then he got hold of a book, or looked at some prints, or chatted with a local worthy, but it was a hard life and they were in narrow circumstances. He grew up among poor people, and he has been called their poet. But he did not like the poor. When he started writing, it was the fashion to pretend that they were happy shepherds and shepherdesses, who were always dancing, or anyhow had hearts of gold. But Crabbe knew the local almshouses and the hospital and the prison, and the sort of people who drift into them ; he read, in the parish registers, the deaths of the unsuccessful, the marriages of the incompetent, and the births of the illegitimate. Though he notes occasional heroism, his general verdict on the working classes is unfavourable. And when he comes to the richer and more respectable inmates of the borough who can veil their defects behind money, he remains sardonic, and sees them as poor people who have not been found out.

He escaped from Aldeborough as soon as he could. His fortunes improved, he won the patronage of Burke, took orders, married well, and ended his life in 1832 in a comfortable west country parsonage. He had done well for himself. Yet he never escaped from Aldeborough in the spirit, and it was the making of him as a poet. Even when he was writing of other things, there steals again and again into his verse the sea, the estuary, the flat Suffolk coast, local meannesses, and an odour of brine and dirt—tempered occasionally with the scent of flowers. We must remember Aldeborough when we read this rather odd poet, for he belongs to the grim little place, and through it to England. And we must remember that though he is an Englishman, he is not a John Bull, and that though he is a clergyman, he is by no means an " old dear."

His poems are easily described and read. They are mostly stories in rhymed couplets, and their subject is local scenes or people. One story will be about the almshouses, another about the vicar, another about inns. " Peter Grimes," which inspires Britten's opera, had an actual original. Another story—the charming " Silford Hall "—tells of a happy visit which a little boy once paid to a country mansion, and how the kind house-keeper showed him round the picture gallery, and gave him a lovely dinner in the servants' hall ; Crabbe had himself been that humble little boy. He is not brilliant or cultivated, witty or townified. He is provincial ; and I am using provincial as a word of high praise.

How good are these stories in verse ? Crabbe is a peculiar writer : some people like him, others don't, and find him dull and even unpleasant. I like him and read him again and again ; and his tartness, his acid humour, his honesty, his feeling for certain English types and certain kinds of English scenery do appeal to me very much. On their account I excuse the absence in him of a warm heart, a vivid imagination, and a grand style : for he has none of those great gifts.

Here are some verses from " Peter Grimes." They show how Crabbe looks at scenery, and how subtly he links the scene with the soul of the observer. The criminal Grimes is already suspected of murdering his apprentices, and no one will go fishing with him in his boat. He rows out alone into the estuary, and waits there—waits for what ?

> When tides were neap, and, in the sultry day,
> Through the tall bounding mud-banks made their way . . .
> There anchoring, Peter chose from man to hide,
> There hang his head, and view the lazy tide
> In its hot slimy channel slowly glide ;

> Where the small eels that left the deeper way
> For the warm shore, within the shallows play ;
> Where gaping muscles, left upon the mud,
> Slope their slow passage to the fallen flood.

How quiet this writing is : you might say how dreary. Yet how sure is its touch ; and how vivid that estuary near Aldeborough.

> Here dull and hopeless he'd lie down and trace
> How sidelong crabs had scrawled their crooked race,
> Or sadly listen to the tuneless cry
> Of fishing gull or clanging golden-eye ;
> What time the sea-birds to the marsh would come,
> And the loud bittern from the bulrush home,
> Gave from the salt ditch side the bellowing boom :
> He nursed the feelings these dull scenes produce,
> And loved to stop beside the opening sluice.

Not great poetry, by any means ; but it convinces me that Crabbe and Peter Grimes and myself do stop beside an opening sluice, and that we are looking at an actual English tideway, and not at some vague, vast imaginary waterfall, which crashes from nowhere to nowhere.

Into this ordinariness, out of the muddy water, rise the spectres—the murdered boys, led by Grimes's father ; and Crabbe, hostile to his own father, leads up to a death-bed of insanity and terror. He is not often so powerful.

> " Still did they force me on the oar to rest,
> And when they saw me fainting and oppress'd,
> He with his hand, the old man, scoop'd the flood,
> And there came flame about him mix'd with blood :
> He bade me stoop and look upon the place,
> Then flung the hot red liquor in my face :
> Burning it blazed, and then I roar'd for pain,
> I thought the demons would have turn'd my brain."
> . . . But here he ceased and gazed
> On all around, affrighten'd and amazed ;
> And still he tried to speak, and look'd in dread
> Of frighten'd females gathering round his bed ;
> Then dropp'd exhausted, and appear'd at rest,
> Till the strong foe the vital powers possess'd ;
> Then with an inward, broken voice he cried,
> " Again they come ! " and mutter'd as he died.

My next quotation is a lighter one. It comes from a malicious poem about the Vicar of the Parish " whose constant care was no man to offend." He begins with a sympathetic description of Aldeborough church, and its lichen-encrusted tower, and now he turns, with less sympathy, to the church's recently deceased incumbent. What a cruel account is this of the Vicar's one and

only love affair ! He had been attracted to a young lady who
lived with her mother ; he called on them constantly, smiling
all the time, but never saying what he was after ; with the
inevitable result that the damsel got tired of her " tortoise," and
gave her hand to a brisker suitor. Thus ended the Vicar's sole
excursion into the realm of passion.

> " I am escaped," he said, when none pursued ;
> When none attack'd him, " I am unsubdued " ;
> " Oh pleasing pangs of love ! " he sang again,
> Cold to the joy, and stranger to the pain.
> E'en in his age would he address the young,
> " I, too, have felt those fires, and they are strong " ;
> But from the time he left his favourite maid,
> To ancient females his devoirs were paid :
> And still they miss him after morning prayer.

He was always " cheerful and in season gay," he gave the
ladies presents of flowers from his garden with mottoes attached ;
he was fond of fishing, he organized charades, he valued friend-
ship, but was not prepared to risk anything for it. One thing
did upset him, and that was innovation ; if the Vicar discovered
anything new, on either the theological or the social horizon,
he grew hot—it was the only time he did get hot.

> Habit with him was all the test of truth :
> " It must be right ; I've done it from my youth."
> Questions he answer'd in as brief a way :
> " It must be wrong : it was of yesterday."
> Though mild benevolence our priest possess'd,
> 'Twas but by wishes or by words express'd.
> Circles in water, as they wider flow,
> The less conspicuous in their progress grow,
> And when at last they touch upon the shore,
> Distinction ceases, and they're view'd no more.
> His love, like that last circle, all embraced,
> But with effect that never could be traced.

The Vicar's fault is weakness, and the analysis and censure
of weakness is a speciality of Crabbe's. His characters postpone
marriage until passion has died ; perhaps this was his own case,
and why he was so bitter about it. Or they marry, and passion
dies because they are too trivial to sustain it. Or they drift
into vice, and do even that too late, so that they are too old to
relish the lustiness of sin. Or like the Vicar they keep to the
straight path because vice is more arduous than virtue. To
all of them, and to their weaknesses, Crabbe extends a little
pity, a little contempt, a little cynicism, and a much larger
portion of reproof. The bitterness of his early experiences has
eaten into his soul, and he does not love the human race,

though he does not denounce it, and dare not despair of its ultimate redemption.

But we must get back to the Vicar, who is awaiting his final epitaph in some anxiety.

> Now rests our Vicar. They who knew him best,
> Proclaim his life t'have been entirely rest ; . . .
> The rich approved,—of them in awe he stood ;
> The poor admired,—they all believed him good ;
> The old and serious of his habits spoke ;
> The frank and youthful loved his pleasant joke ;
> Mothers approved a safe contented guest,
> And daughters one who back'd each small request : . . .
> No trifles fail'd his yielding mind to please,
> And all his passions sunk in early ease ;
> Nor one so old has left this world of sin,
> More like the being that he entered in.

For the Vicar died as a child, who retains his innocence because he has never gained any experience.

These two poems, " Peter Grimes " and " The Vicar " represent the tragic and the satirical side of Crabbe. He is never romantic. Charming at first sight is this picture of the warm-blooded sailor who sets out to win a girl because he has been told he is beneath her. But the chase ends in squalor.

> His trusty staff in his bold hand he took,
> Like him and like his frigate, heart of oak ;
> Fresh were his features, his attire was new ;
> Clean was his linen, and his jacket blue ;
> Of finest jean his trousers, tight and trim ;
> Brush'd the large buckle at the silver rim.
>   He soon arrived, he traced the village green,
> There saw the maid, and was with pleasure seen ;
> Then talk'd of love. . . .

The sailor dies in battle, the girl is disowned of her father, the Parish Clerk enters another bastard in the Register.

> No lads nor lasses came
> To grace the rite, or give the child a name :
> Nor grave conceited nurse, of office proud,
> Bore the young Christian roaring through the crowd.
> In a small chamber was my office done. . . .

Melancholy mists invade the scene. The warm blooded, like the wicked, and like the prudent, have failed.

Crabbe's personality is definitely unattractive. For this his upbringing and his epoch were partly responsible ; he was not quite the gentleman, which he regretted, and Burns had not yet exempted literary men from this particular form of remorse. And he suffered from moral gaucherie also : he disapproved, he reproved. Wherever he looked, he saw human beings taking the wrong turning. This advantaged his art. Disapproval is all too common in the pulpit, but it is rare in poetry, and its presence gives his work a curious flavour, subtle yet tart, which will always attract connoisseurs. We take a bite from an unusual fruit. We come away neither nourished nor ravished, yet aware of a new experience, which we can repeat at will. Were Crabbe insincere, we should not return, but disapproval is as genuine in his hand as indignation in Carlyle's, and, like Carlyle, he never hesitates to turn his weapon against himself. An unusual atmosphere results : it is, so to speak, sub-Christian : there is an implication throughout of positive ideals, such as self-sacrifice and asceticism, but they are rarely pressed ; only occasionally does the narrator let himself testify. As a rule, he prefers to shake his finger at men as they move by wrong paths from the cradle to the grave, and to remind himself with a frown that he, too, is human—a frown that is almost a sigh :

> It is a lovely place, and at the side
> Rises a mountain rock in rugged pride,
> And in that rock are shapes of shells and forms
> Of creatures in old worlds, of nameless worms,
> Whose generations lived and died ere man,
> A worm of other class, to crawl began.

A worm with an immortal soul no doubt, but he never stresses this, for his muse, like his church, discouraged enthusiasm.

Crabbe is not one of our great poets. But he is unusual, he is straight, and he is entirely of England. Aldeborough stamped him for ever. His life was written by the George Crabbe who was his son ; modest, truthful, and sensitive, it is one of the best biographies in our language.[1]

[Reprinted, with alterations and additions, from *The Listener* for May 29th, 1941.]

[1] Recently reprinted in *The World's Classics*.

BY MONTAGU SLATER

The Story of the Opera

The Characters :

PETER GRIMES, a fisherman
ELLEN ORFORD, the Borough schoolmistress
AUNTIE, landlady of The Boar
NIECE I
NIECE 2
BALSTRODE, a retired sea-captain
NED KEENE, an apothecary
BOB BOLES, a Methodist fisherman
MRS. SEDLEY, a widow
SWALLOW, a lawyer
THE RECTOR
DR. THORP
HOBSON, the village carrier
A BOY, Grimes's new apprentice
THE PEOPLE OF THE BOROUGH

CRABBE disliked Peter Grimes. His tale comes in the section called " The Poor " in the long poem " The Borough," in which piece by piece, trades, professions, churches, pubs, clubs, we learn most of what there is to know about the daily existence of a Suffolk fishing and shipbuilding town. Much as Crabbe disliked Peter Grimes, he made him the most romantic character in " The Borough." I doubt whether Crabbe would have admitted this. I believe his dislike of Peter Grimes was genuine. Probably it would have angered him to be told he had made the bad man of the story into a village Byron. Yet this vein appears in almost the first lines about Peter's childhood :

> How when the father in his Bible read
> He in contempt and anger left the shed ;
> " It is the word of life," the parent cried :
> " This is the life itself," the boy replied.

Later, when he comes to Peter's mad brooding on the Alde-

borough scene, Crabbe is roused to an eloquence he does not
often allow himself to use.

Peter Grimes seems to have been the first to introduce into
the Borough the early nineteenth century system of buying
workhouse apprentices, since his pride—and his Byronism—
kept him alone. It takes two people at least to work an
Aldeborough fishing boat. This meant—there was no way out
of it—a hard, cruel life for the boy. But this, as Crabbe half
complains, did not much worry the Borough :

> None put the question, " Peter, dost thou give
> The boy his food ?—What man ! the lad must live :
> Consider, Peter, let the child have bread,
> He'll serve thee better if he's stroked and fed."
> None reasoned thus—and some, on hearing cries,
> Said calmly, " Grimes is at his exercise."

The cruelty of the apprentice system, which soon after Crabbe's
time became characteristic right through England, did not
rouse the Borough at first, though it perturbed Crabbe. In the
Peter Grimes's workshop the cruelty was carried to extremes.
One of the boys died.

This is where the opera begins. The inquest on the death of
Peter's first apprentice—the opera's prologue—turns almost into
Peter's trial. By now the Borough is truly roused. Yet, when
you go into things, it is not quite as simple as it seemed. The
position of a bought apprentice with a fisherman who lives
alone in a hut built out of an upturned boat is intolerable
for both parties, even without intentional cruelty—intolerable
enough to produce the sort of breakdown in which sooner or
later there will be intentional cruelty as well. Yet what else is
a Peter Grimes to do ? He can marry perhaps if he can make
a little money and establish himself. And here, naturally, his
mad pride gets in the way again and Peter Grimes is not one to
creep back apologetically into Borough society. He will come
back in a big way or not at all. He begins with a hinted charge
of murder to live down.

This, then, is the situation in the Coroner's Court in the Moot
Hall. The cross-examinations have a background of mutterings
in the crowd :

> When women gossip the result
> Is someone doesn't sleep at night.
> And then the Crowner sits upon it
> But who can dare to fix the guilt.

There is a moment at the end when Peter, becoming perhaps
for the first time truly aware of his own situation, cries out to
Coroner Swallow :

> Stand down you say. You wash your hands.
> The case goes on in people's minds
> And charges that no court has made
> Will be shouted at my head.
> Let me speak, let me stand trial,
> Bring the accusers to the hall.
> O let me thrust into their mouths
> The truth, the pity and the truth.

It has come out in evidence that he has a friend in court, the widowed schoolmistress of the Borough, Mrs. Ellen Orford. She it was who helped him to carry away from the boat the dead body of his first apprentice after the disastrous failure of his attempt to sail to the London market with a record catch. At the end of the inquest she stays behind with him in the Moot Hall.

ELLEN : Peter come home——
PETER : Home ! Where the walls themselves
      Gossip of inquest !
ELLEN : But we will gossip too,
      And eat and rest.
PETER : While Peeping Toms
      Watch where you go !
      You'll share the name
      Of outlaw too.

The duet in which Ellen tries to comfort Peter and win him from his despairing mood is the end of the Prologue.

After that the opera proper begins—with ",The Borough." An ordinary morning—any morning—but a few days later. The fishermen are hauling in their boats, their wives are mending the nets, the children are playing in the harbour. The parson, the doctor, the lady-gossip come down to the High Street in mid-morning. The landlady of The Boar, a pub of low character, shouts pleasantries from her front door.

The opening chorus summarizing all this, and the final chorus at the end of Act III are the only places in the opera where I have used a direct quotation from Crabbe.

> O hang at open doors the net, the cork,
> While squalid sea-dames at their mending work.
> Welcome the hour when fishing through the tide
> The weary husband throws his freight aside.
>
> O cold and wet and driven with the tide
> Beat your tired arms against your tarry side.
> Find rest in public bars where fiery gin
> Will aid the warmth that languishes within.
>
> Dabbling on shore half-naked sea-boys crowd,
> Swim round a ship, or swing upon a shroud :
> Or in a boat purloined with paddles play
> And grow familiar with the watery way.

It is spring and the Borough is on that part of the east coast where the encroachment of the sea makes coast erosion and landslides a real danger if gales swell the high tides of the equinox. There is watchfulness. There is an air of expectancy. A retired ship's-captain, Balstrode, appoints himself unofficial weather-watcher and sits with his glass on the breakwater waiting for the signs of the wind-change that may bring floods. Peter Grimes has been fishing with the rest, for the first time since the inquest. The business of hauling in his boat becomes the test of whether he can work alone and whether he will get enough—or any—friendly assistance. When he first calls for somebody to give a hand the fishermen turn their backs.

And when Balstrode and Ned Keene, the quack of The Borough, come to his rescue, Keene, who has a sharp nose for a deal, offers a solution :

> Grimes, you won't need help from now,
> I've got a prentice for you.

Later he tells more about it.

KEENE : I called at the workhouse yesterday.
All you do now is fetch the boy.
We'll send the carrier with a note.
He'll bring your bargain on his cart.
[Calls off.
Jim Hobson, we've a job for you.

[Carrier HOBSON *enters.*
HOBSON : Cart's full, sir. More than I can do.
KEENE : Listen, Jim. You'll go to the workhouse
And ask for Mr. Ned Keene's purchase.
Bring him back to Grimes.
HOBSON :   I have no room.
KEENE : Hobson, you'll do what is to be done.
[It is near enough to an argument to attract a crowd. Fishermen and
women gather round, including BOB BOLES.
BOLES : Is this a Christian country when
Workhouse children are such slaves,
Their souls and bodies go for cash ?
KEENE : Hobson. Will you do your job ?
HOBSON : I have to go from pub to pub,
Picking up parcels, standing about.
The journey back is late at night.
Mister, find some other road
To bring your boy back.
CROWD :   He's afraid.
HOBSON : Mister, find some other road.

> *[*ELLEN ORFORD *has come in. She is a widow of about forty. Her*
> *children have died, or grown up and gone away, and in her loneliness*
> *she has become the Borough schoolmistress. A hard life has not*
> *hardened her. It has made her more charitable.*

ELLEN :   Carter, I'll mind your passenger.
CROWD :   What ?   And be Grimes's messenger ?
ELLEN :   Whatever you say I'm not ashamed.
           Somebody must do the job.
           The carter goes from pub to pub,
           Picking up parcels, standing about.
           The boy needs comfort late at night,
           He needs a welcome on the road
           Coming here strange.   He'll be afraid.
KEENE :   Mrs. Orford is talking sense.
CROWD :   Ellen, you're leading us a dance
           Fetching a boy for Peter Grimes.
                [Underneath there is a general mutter of comment.   It resolves itself into :
CHORUS :   Because the Borough is afraid
           She who helps will share the blame.

Ellen answers in an *aria.*

ELLEN :   Let him among you without fault
           Cast the first stone.
           And let the Pharisees and Saducees
           Give way to none.

           But whosoever feels his pride
           Humbled so deep
           There is no corner he can hide
           Even in sleep.

           Will have no trouble to find out
           How a poor teacher
           Widowed and lonely finds delight
           In shouldering care.
                [She breaks off.
           Mr. Hobson, where's your cart ?
           I'm ready.
HOBSON :   Here, ma'am.   I can wait.

I have reproduced here a couple of pages of the libretto partly as the quickest way of telling the story, partly to show the form it is written in, four-beat half-rhymed verse, as conversational as possible and not too regular—with indeed other irregularities in the recitative brought in by the music, some of which I have ignored in the page quoted.   That is to say here and there the composer will drop half a line or repeat one and temporarily break up the half-rhyme scheme, producing an even more conversational effect.   Then, as feelings rise, the momentary situation will be crystallized in an aria in any measure, sometimes rhymed and sometimes half-rhymed.   At some places too we come to what the composer calls " a half number."   An example of that is in the lines first spoken by Hobson and later repeated by Ellen :

           I have to go from pub to pub,
           Picking up parcels, standing about.
           The journey back is late at night.

and so on to the end of the paragraph. This, as you will find,
without quite breaking away from the frame of the recitative
develops a little tune of its own.

Thus the main situation is set. Peter is going to start again
with a new apprentice, Ellen is going to help this time. And the
Borough fears the worst. The Borough gets the worst for the
moment, insofar as Balstrode's expected wind-change happens
just near high spring-tide and flood is certain. The storm breaks
soon after Ellen and Hobson have set off for Ipswich in the
carrier's cart to fetch, among other things, Grimes's apprentice.
Before the end of the scene Balstrode—who in general plays the
part of the detached and kindly observer—has singled out Peter
Grimes and put a question to him. Is this taking too much risk?
Isn't it starting the same story over again—though with a new
apprentice? Why doesn't he go away, perhaps into the Merchant
Navy? Grimes says:

> I'm a provincial, rooted here.
> BALSTRODE : Rooted by what?
> PETER : By familiar fields,
> Mudbanks, sand,
> Ordinary streets,
> The prevailing wind.

They talk as the storm rises, and in their talk we get something
of the other side of Grimes, Grimes the ambitious, Grimes the
man of enterprise. Mocked, and, as he thinks, hardly treated
by the Borough, he's going to show them what he's made of.
He's going to make his pile, somehow, anyhow, if that is all the
Borough is capable of taking notice of. When he's done that
he'll marry Ellen and set up house, home, and shop. It is a
fierce, self-destructive energy, echoed by the storm now rising
to its climax.

The second scene of Act I takes place later the same night in
The Boar where news comes piecemeal of flooded roads and
eroded coast including a fall of cliff just behind Grimes's hut.
The hut is undisturbed, but part of the cliff behind it has been
carried away. One of those waiting in The Boar is an incongruous figure, a widow rentier, Mrs. Sedley—incongruous
because The Boar is a disreputable place and a byword for the
landlady's regular supply of so-called nieces. Mrs. Sedley is
waiting anxiously for Hobson to bring back her supply of
laudanum which she buys privately—but not secretly, since
laudanum-taking was common enough in these days—through
Ned Keene. At last, wet, late, and dishevelled, Ellen, the
carrier, and the boy arrive and, through the storm, Peter takes
him home.

Act II begins on a Sunday morning some weeks later. It is peaceful now and

> The sun in
> His fair morning
> And upward climb
> Makes the world warm.

Morning prayers are beginning in the Borough Parish Church. Outside Ellen and the boy are sunning themselves, Ellen quietly chatting to the boy.

> Shall we forget this is a Sunday
> And do our knitting by the sea ?
>
> I'll do the work. You talk.
>
> Nothing to tell me ? Then shall I
> Guess what your life was like and you
> Tell me if I go wrong ?
>
> I believe
> You liked your workhouse and its grave
> Empty look. You liked to be
> A lonely fellow in your misery.
>
> When I became a teacher
> I thought of school first as a chore,
> Then found it the sort of place—
> I daresay like your own workhouse—
> Where the woes of little people
> Hurt more, but are more simple.

People are going to church. We overhear some of the service. Of course Mrs. Sedley gets to church late and on her way in she sees something of what follows.

What follows is first Ellen's discovery that the boy's shirt-neck is torn and his neck bruised. He won't tell why. Then Peter arrives breaking up the holiday atmosphere with a demand that the boy puts on his working clothes and comes away. There is a shoal.

ELLEN : But if there were then all the boats
    Would be fast launching.
PETER : I can see
    The signs before another eye.

There begins one of those quarrels which, starting from a commonplace pretext, tower quickly into passionate self-examination and self-justification. Ellen asks about the boy's bruises, argues that in any case they have an agreement about the boy that he stays with her on Sundays. We see again Peter's

self-destroying energy, his—and it's the key-word of the period
—enterprise.   Ellen reasons with him about just this.

> Peter, your unforgiving work,
> This grey, unresting industry,
> What aim, what future does it mark?
> What peace will your hard profits buy?

Peter flares up.   Both lose their tempers.

ELLEN : Peter, tell me one thing, where
            The youngster got his ugly bruise.
PETER : Out of the hurly-burly.
ELLEN :   O your ways
            Are hard and rough beyond his days.
            Peter, we're wrong in what we planned
            To do, we're wrong.
PETER :   Take away your hand.
            [*Then quietly.*
            My only hope depends on you.
            If you—take it away—what's left?
ELLEN : We were mistaken when we schemed
            To solve your life by lonely toil.
            We were mistaken when we hoped
            That you'd come through and all be well.

            Peter, you cannot buy your peace.
            You'll never stop the gossips' tale
            With all the shoals from all the seas.
            Peter, we should give in. We've failed.
            [*He cries out as if in agony.   Then strikes her.   Her basket falls.*
PETER : So be it.   And God have mercy upon me.
            [*The boy runs from him and* PETER *follows.*

Behind closed doors and half-open windows neighbours have
been watching.   Some of them now emerge, among them
Auntie (landlady of The Boar) and Ned Keene the quack.

AUNTIE : Fool to let it come to this,
               Wasting pity, squandering tears.
NED :   See the glitter in his eyes,
               Grimes is at his exercise.

Morning prayers are over and the church parade begins.
The crowd joins in the gossip and hubbub about these events
(some of which Mrs. Sedley, coming late to church, has witnessed
along with the non-churchgoers).   Presently, in the crowd, Bob
Boles makes a speech of indignation.

BOLES : People—no, I *will* speak—people !
               This thing here concerns you all.
BALSTRODE : Tub-thumping——— !
BOLES :   O this prentice system
               Is uncivilized, unchristian.
BALSTRODE : Something of the sort befits
                       Brats conceived outside the sheets

BOLES : Where's the parson in his black?
        Is he there, or is he not
        To guide a sinful straying flock?

It grows into a public scene. The Rector is brought into it unwillingly. Ellen is fetched and asked what she has been doing. " Popular feeling's rising," as the Rector puts it, and presently the outcome is that the Rector, Swallow, and others lead the way to Grimes's hut to find out what is going on.

While they are on the way the scene changes to Grimes's hut, with Peter and the boy.

PETER : Here's your sea-boots. Take those bright
        And fancy buckles off your feet.
        Here's your oil-skin and sou'wester.
        Stir your pins, we must get ready.
        Here's the jersey that she knitted,
        With the anchor that she patterned.

At first he is grim and rough, urging the boy on.

        Look. We'll make a record catch.
        The whole sea's boiling. Get the nets.
        Come John.

Then there comes an echo of his earlier self-persuasion.

        They listen to money,
        These Borough gossips.
        Into the shoal now.
        Swamp their markets.
        Sell the good catches.
        Get money to choke
        Down rumour's throat.
        That wealthy merchant
        Grimes will set up—
        You will all see it—
        With house and home and shop.
        I'll marry Ellen.
        I'll . . .

All this is a quotation from his argument with Balstrode in the first act. It all comes back to him, but with a memory behind it of Ellen's unforgivable phrase : " Peter, we should give in. We've failed." The thought changes his mood to something more wistful. He thinks aloud in the presence of the boy.

PETER : My thinking builds for us some kindlier home,
        Warm in my heart and in a golden calm
        Where there is no more fear and no more storm.
        And you would soon forget your workhouse ways,
        Forget the labour of our weary days,
        Wrapped round in kindness like September haze.

But thinking builds what thinking can disown.
Dead fingers are stretched out to tear it down.
I hear my father and the one that drowned

Calling, There is no peace, there is no stone
In the earth's thickness to make you a home,
That you can build with and remain alone.
[*He stops. The boy watches him in fascinated horror : and* PETER
turns on him suddenly.
Sometimes I see two devils in this hut ;
They're here now by the cramp under my heart—
My father and the boy I had
As prentice until you arrived.
They sit there and their faces shine like flesh.
Their mouths are open, but I close my ears.

He hears the Borough coming up the hill. He looks out to see
who it is and decides to get away before they come. The boat
is moored at the foot of the cliff just behind the hut—where the
landslide was in the spring floods. He flings down his nets and
ropes from the cliff-side door, urging the boy to scramble after
them. (We can still hear the Borough approaching.) The
boy goes out, but as he starts to climb down the cliff he slips and
falls. We hear him scream as he disappears. Peter scrambles
down the cliff after him. When the Rector and the Coroner
and the rest of the people of the Borough arrive they find the
hut neat and empty, though the cliff-side door is open. They
look round the hut first, then out of the door.

RECTOR :   Was this a recent landslide ?
SWALLOW :   Yes.
RECTOR :   It makes almost a precipice.
            How deep ?
SWALLOW :   Say fifty feet.
RECTOR :   Dangerous to have the door open.
KEENE :   He used to keep his boat down there.
            Maybe they've both gone fishing.
RECTOR :   Yet
            His hut is reasonably kept.
            Here's order. Here is skill.
SWALLOW :   The whole affair gives Borough talk its—shall
            I say quietus ? Here we come pell-mell
            Expecting to find out we know not what,
            And all we find's a neat and empty hut.
            Gentlemen, take this lesson to your wives,
            " Less interference in our private lives."
RECTOR :   There's no point certainly in staying here.
            Will the last comer please to close the door ?

This is the end of Act II.
The last act brings us back to the Borough—a summer
evening, and one of the season's subscription dances is taking
place in the Moot Hall. It is three days later. Almost every-

body we have met at the Borough is either at the dance or at
The Boar—and there is a constant passage between the two.
So we pick up the news and gossip. Peter Grimes has not been
seen since Sunday—nor the boy. Mrs. Sedley suspects murder
and has a clue. At a moment when everybody else is inside,
Balstrode and Ellen walk up from the harbour. Balstrode has
fetched her because he has noticed (everybody else has been
too busy) that Peter Grimes's boat has been pulled up on to
the shore. Apparently he has come back. And Ellen has found
down by the latest tidemark the jersey on which she had
embroidered an anchor for the boy. They talk about Peter.

BALSTRODE : We'll find him, maybe give him a hand.
ELLEN : He's walked out of the human world.
We have no power to help him now.
BALSTRODE : We have the power. We have the power.

Their discovery of the return of Grimes's boat is repeated by Mrs.
Sedley, and the fact becoming generally known, Swallow instructs
Hobson—as constable—to take a posse of men and find Grimes.
We hear them shouting as they go out with their lanterns.

The last scene begins in the small hours of the same morning.
A sea-fog has come up. Peter has come back to the middle of
the Borough. He has been alone for three days, hungry, wet,
frenzied, almost insane. Ellen—and later Balstrode—find him.
It is Balstrode who proposes the solution—that he takes his
boat out, scuttles it and goes down with it. Peter does what
he is told and Balstrode leads Ellen away.

Dawn begins to break. Day comes to the Borough by a
gentle sequence of sights and sounds. A candle is lighted and
shines through a bare window. A shutter is drawn back.

Hobson and his posse meet severally by the Moot Hall. They
gossip together, shake their heads, indicate the hopelessness of
the search, extinguish their lanterns, and while some turn home
others go to the boats. Nets are brought down from the houses
by fisherwives. Cleaners open the front door of the Inn and
begin to scrub the step. The doctor comes from a confinement
case. The Rector—followed by Mrs. Sedley—comes to early
morning prayer. Swallow brings a rumour :

SWALLOW : There's a boat sinking out at sea
Coastguard reports.
FISHERMAN : Within reach ?
SWALLOW : No.
[BOLES looks through his glass.
AUNTIE : What is it ?
BOLES : Nothing I can spy.
AUNTIE : One of these rumours.

The day's work begins in the Borough. It is described in the big final chorus, taken up by more and more people as the street becomes repopulated. Like the first chorus it is a direct quotation from Crabbe.

> To those who pass, the Borough's bells betray
> The cold beginning of another day,
> And houses sleeping by the waterside
> Wake to the measured ripple of the tide :
>
> Or measured cadence of the lads who tow
> Some entered hoy to fix her in her row,
> Or hollow sound that from the passing bell
> To some departed spirit bids farewell.
>
> In ceaseless motion comes and goes the tide.
> Flowing it fills the channel vast and wide,
> Then back to sea with strong, majestic sweep
> It rolls in ebb yet terrible and deep.

I ought to add in fairness to Crabbe that the story as worked out in the opera uses Crabbe's poem only as a starting-point. Crabbe produced character sketches of some of the main persons of the drama. I have taken these character sketches as clues and woven them into a story against the background of the Borough : but it is my story and the composer's (the idea was originally not mine but Britten's), and I have to take the responsibility for its shape as well as its words. I can't blame Crabbe !

BY EDWARD SACKVILLE-WEST

The Musical and Dramatic Structure

DRAMA is inherent in the nature of all musical compositions, but the drama of a symphony is different both in degree and in kind from the drama of certain songs, or of opera. Symphonic development can be—and, since Wagner, often has been—used in opera ; but its use within a symphonic movement obeys the form of that movement and is otherwise dictated by the nature of the themes. The symphony is a closed world, fulfilling itself and self-sufficient all along the line, whatever the circumstances (cortex of emotions, world-picture, or whatnot) that sowed the seed of it. Opera, on the other hand, leans on the articulate emotion and must follow a sequence of *verbal* thought. Open on to the world of language, music renounces the heaven peculiar to itself for the sake of illuminating the earthly and the contingent. The price it has to pay for this feat has sometimes been over-estimated by composers themselves ; and *Fidelio, L'Africaine, La Forza del Destino, Lohengrin,* and *Strauss, Salome,* are various but all superior examples of the uneasiness which results from word and song married on incompatible grounds. In each case words and music win alternately, at each other's expense : an inadmissible state of affairs. Something more than a faulty method is here involved—though that has much to do with our dissatisfaction, our sense of fine material disadvantageously handled : we feel, I believe, some fundamental lack of cohesion between the two orders—that of the drama and that of the music. What should have become a single world—opera, in fine—has remained two.

The problem can be solved in one of two ways : the words can be sacrificed, as in *Tristan* (although Wagner pretended to think otherwise), and the musical form and texture enormously elaborated and magnified to compensate for the loss ; or the music—both voices and orchestra—may be subordinated to the text, as in *Falstaff* and above all *Pelléas et Mélisande.* In the first case the orchestra becomes the chief vehicle of communication, in the second the voice. On the one hand, then, music-drama ; on the other, opera.

Peter Grimes is an opera. Before enlarging on this statement,

it will be as well to sketch in those features of the composer's
development which seem to have led up to this work. Benjamin
Britten's interest in the dramatic energies of music reaches some
way back into his career. The two concertos, the *Scottish
Ballad*, and even more the *Sinfonia da Requiem*, are essentially
dramatic in effect; and even so purely musical a work as
the *Prelude and Fugue for Strings* is executed according to a
plan which regards the world of sound as an instrument
of histrionic eloquence. In these works Britten discovered
and explored his orchestra; the solo violin and piano in the
concertos serving, in some degree, to elucidate the expressive
possibilities of the single voice. But *Les Illuminations*, the
Michelangelo Sonnets, and the *Serenade*, bring us right up to the
threshold of opera : the technique, the method, the approach,
are already those of *Peter Grimes*. In the *Sonnets* the voice-line
is far more deliberately Italianate than any Britten had
uttered before or since; but the bareness of the accompaniment and the concentration of melody — and indeed of all
expression—in the voice alone, reflect the composer's fundamental attitude to song. Where words are present, notes must
follow and throw into relief, not drown or distort them or
subordinate them to the orchestral symphony. And even in
Les Illuminations and the *Serenade*, where each movement is
less a song (in the accepted sense of the word) than a *scena*,
the centre of interest only shifts from the voice during its
moments of silence. In the *Serenade*, Britten's setting of
Blake's elegy, " O Rose, thou art sick," is a succinct epitome of
the composer's operatic style and foreshadows, with arresting
completeness, the opera which was already in his mind. So in
Peter Grimes we expect to find the melodic line following the
natural rise and fall of the voice in *speaking* a phrase or sentence ;
and this is what happens. We notice also that the vowels, being
given the equivalent of their natural length in note values, do
not " sound silly " as sung English—especially recitative—so
often does, when the note values represent open Italian or
German vowels, instead of the closed ones of our own tongue.

Much has been written both for and against opera as a form
of art, but one thing is certain : no composer who has not
mastered music, in all its aspects, can hope to be successful in a
medium which involves so strenuous a conjugation of all his
musical faculties. He need not have published a symphony or
a string quartet, but if he has not mastered the technique of
symphonic development and of lucid part-writing, he will
approach his libretto without adequate means to handle the
various and inevitable connections between the parts of each

scene and act, or the ability to manage so complex a texture and balance as opera continuously involves. A good opera, then, represents the composer at the height of his powers : it must always be a result, never a point of departure (except for future operas). It is a bourne from which the traveller may return, but with an outlook necessarily changed by the experience.

Benjamin Britten has served a long apprenticeship, but the tendency of his imagination, as his recent works show, has long been in the direction of the word-music texture and therefore, ultimately, of opera.

Of opera, not music-drama ; for Britten is not the rhapsodic kind of composer : he thinks in terms of clear-cut units and of how they can be combined in an organic whole. Thus *Peter Grimes* is full of musical images which describe what is going on, either in the minds of the characters or on the stage (see Ex. 5 and 7), but there are no motifs in the Wagnerian sense. With the exception of one short but crucial scene in the third act, the opera is through-composed : the music is quite continuous and there are no full closes within the acts. Nevertheless each scene is divided, according to the course of events, into a number of recognizable units. This makes the opera relatively simple to analyse, since each unit is describable in terms of a separate musical form and any complications that occur can be resolved into their components without confusing the analysis or betraying the organization.

I think it is not an exaggeration to say that, except when the curtain is down, the musical interest is throughout confined to the voices. During dialogue, the orchestra merely comments ; in arias and other concerted passages it takes no more upon itself than is needed to complete the emotion. In fine, the orchestra *accompanies* the voices, leaving to them the burden of expression. This concentration of melodic interest in the voices enables the ear to receive the full impact of the orchestra when it is set free—*i.e.*, in the preludes to the three acts and the interludes between the scenes. All these are, within their concise limits, fully symphonic ; and their aim is impressionistic. Calm weather, sunlight on little waves, tempest on the sea and in the mind, an empty village street under a windless moon ; finally, the mists that creep up from the sea and into Grimes's desperate heart, congealing there into a suicidal resolve : these are the tasks that fall to the orchestra unaided.

Britten's scoring has always been conspicuous for lucidity ; in this opera it is particularly spare and simple, though the tone-colour is in places very startling and unusual. But such

word - music   v   music - drama

effects are arrived at by imaginative combinations of two or
three instruments or groups, rather than by a complicated
mixture of tones such as we find in the scores of Richard Strauss.
So that the orchestra used in *Peter Grimes* is, by operatic stan-
dards of the past sixty years, modest ; it is, in fact, the orchestra
of the later Verdi operas.

It is no part of my present task to extol *Peter Grimes* at the
expense of other operas—still less to suggest that Benjamin
Britten will never write a better. The object of this essay is
henceforward simply the exposition of a musico-dramatic
structure, and if some criticism has been inevitable in these
preliminary remarks, I hope to exclude it altogether from what
follows.

PROLOGUE

The opera plunges at once *in medias res*, the curtain rising
after seven bars in which the wood-wind announces a busy
theme that is later sung by Swallow to the words : " Peter
Grimes, I here advise you : do not take another boy apprentice."

Example 1.ᵃ

the gossip theme

Example 1.ᵇ

Since it is all-important that the facts of the trial should
reach the audience as clearly as possible, the whole of this
scene is composed of recitative, accompanied by short and sharp
orchestral comment in the style of Ex. 1 (*a*), and by the chorus
of villagers, whose role here is to emphasize the phases of the
trial, and, by drowning Grimes whenever he attempts an
explanation, to give credence to his complaints of " gossip and
interference." The pattern of these choral interruptions consists
of a semiquaver figure (Ex. 1 (*b*)) for flutes and bassoons, with
the voices building up chords sustained by the horn quartet in
the middle parts.

This material, split up, truncated, and combined in many
different ways, suffices to generate the climax of the scene,
where Grimes attempts, for the last time, to make himself heard

above the persistent quavers of the chorus and Hobson's demand that the court be cleared. Here the strings and tuba quietly sustain the harmony, while a bassoon, a clarinet, and a flute pass the " gossip " theme (Ex. 1 (b)) to and fro, weaving a rope tighter and tighter round Grimes's call for " the pity, and the truth." At last, to a fortissimo statement of Ex. 1 (a), the court is cleared, and as the theme gradually disintegrates and dies into silence, the court-room empties, leaving Grimes and Ellen alone.

The ensuing duet is unaccompanied and *senza misura*. At first broken and tentative, the two voices answer one another in different but closely related keys—Ellen in E major, Grimes in F minor. Grimes's refusal to be comforted is represented by his own repetition of Ellen's phrases, but with F instead of E ; while the underlying sympathy which binds them is symbolically contained in the A flat enharmonically common to both keys. Gradually, as Grimes gives way to Ellen's entreaty, their voices approach one another and overlap in closer and closer counterpoint, until at last they break in unison into a broad arioso in E major which brings the scene to a close, *lento e tranquillo*. As the curtain descends, the orchestra enters once more.

The interlude which follows is, properly speaking, the Prelude to the opera, and it is constructed from the following sequence

Example 2

Lento e tranquillo

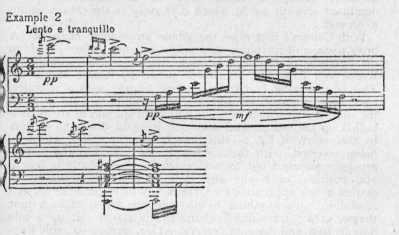

expatiated upon in a free symphonic manner and attaining a rich climax with a sequence of diatonic chords scored for brass, by the whole orchestra. This structure of diatonic thirds

establishes a calm, everyday atmosphere and prepares us for
what is going on at the rise of the curtain on

ACT I

Scene 1

For the first 138 bars of this scene—until the entry of Grimes
—Ex. 2 continues to dominate the score. The chorus, in unison,
sings a square and sturdy tune, and all the while we hear, in
the fragmentary arpeggios, the tranquil sea lapping against the
boats in the harbour. Apart from the choral tune, the musical
interest of this deliberately static scene resides in the tonal
ambiguity—the constant drifting backwards and forwards
between A major and A minor, with here and there a hint of
D major. The characters, as they come into the picture, vary
the texture of the material slightly, but without changing its
shape. At the mention of a storm on the horizon, muted
trombones hold a deep major seventh ; but the moment passes,
the twinkling calm of Ex. 2 returns, and the fisherfolk continue
their song. The tempo quickens a little as Mrs. Sedley enters,
and a jerky theme from the double basses suggests Auntie's
easy good humour ; but once again the fundamental
structure reimposes itself, only to be resolved into a
dominant seventh on A, which dies away as the chorus comes
to an end.

With Grimes's first note, the whole atmosphere changes. A
brisk passage of recitative in six-eight measure (*allegro*) leads to
the beaching of Grimes's boat—a short concerted number for
Keene and Balstrode, afterwards joined by Auntie and Boles.
This is a heaving barcarolle (*andante pesante*) with a relentless
bass, horn portamento, and a single xylophone note to stress
the rhythm. It comes to a noisy and abrupt end as the boat is
pulled up the beach, and attention is again drawn to Grimes
by the return of Ex. 2—this time creating a sinister effect by
being inverted, with the minims in the bass and the watery
arpeggio, shrieked out by a clarinet, more emphatic in length
and position, as Keene and Boles discuss the possibility of
getting a new apprentice for Grimes. With Hobson the carter's
refusal to have anything to do with the transaction, a new
theme, of a " travelling " character, is announced by a solo
double bass and bassoon, *pesante*. This, combined with fragments of Ex. 2, forms the basis of a short episode, in which the
chorus and Ellen join, the former in support of Hobson, the
latter attempting to persuade the carter to give way. When

this episode reaches a climax, Ellen interrupts it with an impassioned *arioso*, trouncing the villagers and taking responsibility on herself. This passage, in D minor and marked *con moto*, is characterized by a scale of sedately descending sixths, scored for strings and accompanied in the bass by a scale in contrary motion. This is answered by wood-wind chords, *pp.*, creating a hymnic effect with their steady crotchet-beat. A considerable climax is built from the alternation of these two sequences, after which the material is allowed to dissolve into the higher registers as Mrs. Sedley asks Hobson if he has brought her sleeping draught. Some ill-natured joking at the poor lady's expense, on the part of oboe, piccolo, and bassoon, assisted by harp reminiscences of Ex. 2, leads to a new episode : the approach of the storm.

Heralded by a return of the major seventh chord, on the lower strings, brass, and percussion, Balstrode announces the theme of what is to become a fully worked-out fugue (*allegro molto*) in G minor for four-part chorus, sextet of solo voices, and full orchestra.

Example 3

At first the fugal entries are confined to the soloists, the chorus filling in the polyphony with exclamatory phrases in syncopated rhythm, supported by wood-wind and brass, while the strings double the solo voices. At the words : " Flooding our seasonal fears," the chorus takes over the theme in unison, handing the counterpoint over to the soloists, and the instrumental texture thickens accordingly. The music traverses a number of keys, climbing higher and higher as the excitement grows, and at the words : " Look ! the storm cone ! " chorus, soloists, and strings together give out the theme, *ff.*, in augmentation, while the lower wind have a syncopated passage in octaves (derived from the introduction to the fugue) which pulls the whole structure downwards into the original key. A *stretta* ensues, sung by Keene and Boles, and accompanied by a trochaic figure for strings alone, later joined by the wind doubling the choral polyphony. This leads to the *coda* : " O tide that waits for no man ! " again delivered in unison by all the voices and interrupted by a violent orchestral passage which plays an important part in the interlude following the scene.

Example 4

This alternation is used to pacify the music as the crowd disperses ; and in the scene which follows, between Grimes and Balstrode, fragments of the storm theme (Ex. 3 and 4) form the basis of the material. The musical development here is very free, and since it follows closely the complex emotions of the two men, it cannot be described in detail. Suffice it to say that the form is accompanied recitative, broadening out into passages of *arioso* wherever dialogue is held up by the images of Grimes's tortured memory. An important passage of this kind begins with Grimes's words : " Picture what my life was like, tied to a child ! whose loneliness, despair, flooded the cabin."

Example 5

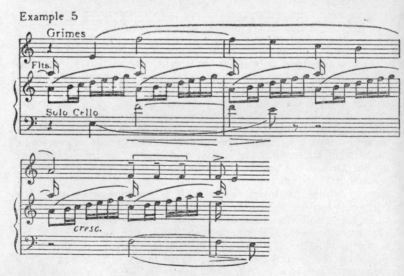

This is pursued to a considerable climax and is followed closely by an extended movement in D, in which Grimes's hatred of the village gossips breaks out once more in a feverish *scherzando* (*Vivace*—six-eight measure). At the climax, the solo becomes a duet, which ends with a return of Ex. 4 as Balstrode goes into The Boar.

Left alone, Grimes launches into a passionate restatement of Ex. 5, this time in the major key and with very full orchestral support ; but the unsteadiness of his feelings allows the tempo to increase until his voice is drowned in a rush of tempestuous quavers. As the curtain descends, the storm at last bursts from the orchestra.

It should be noticed that the music of this interlude is a developed piece and not a mere elaboration of passage-work. The storm themes were chosen for their susceptibility to symphonic treatment, so that, instead of mere static noise and ado, this is a true movement which follows, not the change of scene, but the progress of the storm itself. When the curtain rises once more, the orchestral gale has become a hurricane, by virtue not of stepped-up dynamics, but of the far intenser drama of purely musical growth, in which an orchestral repetition of Grimes's final outburst plays an important part.

Scene 2

From the rise of the curtain on the interior of The Boar, to the entry of Grimes, twenty-five pages later, the musical structure of this scene does not call for close analysis. The orchestra, which represents the storm, is virtually excluded by the cosiness of the pub and is only able to get in when one of the characters (and they all enter in course of the scene) opens the door—until Grimes brings the storm in with him, after which it stays there, setting the pace and character of the music.

At first the dialogue is carried on in very rapid recitative, *senza misura*, accompanied only by a single percussion instrument (bass drum, side drum, cymbals, harp, tambourine, as the case may be) which performs a roll *ad lib.* until the door of the inn opens to admit somebody, when an excited orchestral outburst (founded on Ex. 3 and 4) occurs, and continues until the actors succeed in shutting the door.

Auntie's rebuke to Balstrode is a short, characteristic piece, in a humorous, galumphing style. It consists of two stanzas, the second repeating the first a semi-tone higher, and each one rounded off by a refrain sung in canon by the nieces and poor Mrs. Sedley who, much agitated by her unaccustomed surroundings, is squeezed into a corner of the room and a minor second from anybody who happens to be near her when she dares to open her mouth.

Boles, by now thoroughly drunk (on one glass), makes florid love to one of the nieces. This brief comic episode leads up to Balstrode's speech : " We live and let live and look we keep our hands to ourselves," which is composed in the same style as Auntie's, and of similar, though more obviously masculine, material ; and it is brought to a sudden end by the usual struggle with the door and a consequent incursion of the storm theme. At the end of the ensuing recitative (accompanied, this time, by the tambourine), the door again opens and Grimes enters, announced by the major seventh chord associated with the storm and blared out by muted horns, while the piccolo holds a shake on A in alt. This is followed by a version of Ex. 5 (with flattened E and B), uttered, *con fuoco*, by the full orchestra, but quickly reduced to a mere *tremolando* on low E, as Mrs. Sedley faints and the chorus whispers : " Talk of the Devil and there he is " in major seconds above it. A remark of Keene's : " Everybody's very quiet ! " clears the ground for Grimes's monologue (" Now the Great Bear and Pleiades "), an *arioso*—again stanzaic in form—which creates the one moment of absolute calm and stillness in the entire scene. The melody, here for once taken away from the voice, is imitated in canon by four groups of strings, proceeding from the bass upwards, thus :

This canon draws the starscape, the image of which is then held in place by a sustained chord for all the strings, until the voice has completed its phrase. At the third repetition, after a brief *animato*, the canonic sequence is inverted and comes to a close on an open E over the whole register. The highest note, however, leads over, by means of a violin tremolo, to a brisk passage of choral counterpoint doubled by wood-wind, the " sprung " rhythm of which expresses the general alarm aroused by Grimes's strange mood. The nieces, and later Boles and Balstrode, top the polyphony, or interrupt it, with exclamatory

The Borough High Street.

Inside "The Boar."

Peter Grimes's Hut.

Peter Grimes.

Ellen Orford.

The Boy Apprentice.

Swallow.

The Rector.

Stiff bonnet
torn black satin
edging — crepe
ruching — torn veil;
attached also to
right side front of
bonnet

Mrs. Sedley.

A Niece.

A Borough Fisherman.

A page of the Manuscript orchestral score.

phrases.   Feeling against Grimes rises.   " Chuck him out ! "
cry the chorus, and Boles adds the last straw by remarking :
" His exercise is not with men but killing boys ! "   To prevent
a fight, Auntie, in a phrase we have heard her sing earlier in the
scene, calls upon someone to " start a song."

    The boisterous Round [1] which follows is the *pièce de résistance*
of the whole scene and deserves close attention for the ingenuity
with which it is composed.   The key is E flat, the measure seven
crotchets in a bar $(2+2+3)$, and there are three distinct
tunes representing three ways of accenting the rhythm.   The
Round is started by Keene, taken up by Auntie, then Balstrode,
the nieces, and Boles.   The accompaniment, to begin with, is a
simple but relentless drum crotchet, and as each voice enters it
is emphasized by a skirl from the flutes.   Here is the material
as it appears by the time all three tunes have got going :

Example 7

After four bars of this even Mrs. Sedley cannot resist entering
the consort ;   and at the end of another " round " the chorus
joins the sextet of soloists.   Not to be outdone, the latter weave
a rope of decorations (the scale of E flat in quavers with a
flattened D) to the words " O haul away ! " and pass it from
one to another.   When the Round, in this final form, has

    [1] " A species of canon in unison, so called because the performers begin the
melody at regular rhythmical periods, and return from its conclusion to its
beginning, so that it continually passes round and round from one to another
of them."   (Edward F. Rimbault, quoted in Grove's *Dictionary*.)

reached the chorus, Grimes (the rebel, the outlaw, the one-who-will-not-fit-in) upsets the course of it by singing the original tune in augmentation. The substructure falls away and the material, substantially reduced but retaining its rhythm, wanders through remote keys until the soloists, joining the chorus in obdurate unison, force the whole thing back into its original key and shape, and Grimes is overwhelmed. The orchestra now joins the Round, churning the whole mixture until it thickens, at white heat, into an immitigable major triad, which is suddenly interrupted as the door opens to admit Ellen, Hobson, and the little boy, Grimes's new apprentice. A thunderous minor ninth from the low brass is resolved into its component notes to form a four-quaver figure which is *ad lib.*'d *pp.* below the ensuing

Example 8

recitative. This, interrupted by snatches of Ex. 4, brings us to the point where Ellen bids the boy go home with Grimes, and the rest of the cast shout " Home ! " derisively on an open fifth. As the man takes the child out into the storm, the orchestra brings down the curtain with a swift and violent coda in E flat minor, based still on Ex. 4.

ACT II

After the terror of the storm and the bodeful excitement attending the arrival of Grimes's new apprentice, the second act opens with a Prelude that sparkles with sunlight reflected from the sea on the weather-beaten stone houses of the little town. Above a series of thirds, which sway backwards and forwards on the horns, the wood-wind execute a gay little *toccata* (Ex. 9).

The syncopation gradually gives way, first to a straight execution of the figure, then to a shake and an upward slide which introduces the violins in a slightly varied repetition of Ex. 9. The flutes make occasional pounces, by way of putting the violins off their stroke, and the end of the sequence leads to

Example 9

a broad, calm tune for violas and cellos in pungent unison. This has only a skeleton accompaniment, but the flutes continue their cheeky incursions until, at the end of the tune, they gather more wood-wind to their aid, and soon the whole orchestra is trilling in superimposed bunches of diatonic thirds reminiscent of the arpeggio in Ex. 2. The *toccata* is now ready to return. It is given out, *fff*., by the trumpets, while the strings romp along with the figure in diminution, and as the merriment approaches its height the church bell (a deep B flat) sends up the curtain on

Scene I

The trilling dies down as Ellen and John (the little apprentice) enter, and with Ellen's first words : "The sun in his own morning," the tune previously given to the cellos and violas returns, this time in D major, with little flute decorations and underpinned by a deep *pp*. chord of B flat, from bassoons, double basses, and tuba. At the end of Ellen's speech a second and higher bell—in E flat—replaces the first, and the organ starts the church service with a sequence of chords founded on the horn thirds with which the act opened. These are interspersed with fragments of the *toccata* theme, *pizzicato*, as Ellen and John sit down on the breakwater, after which the upper strings meditate on the tune in canon, until the bell stops.

The *scena* which follows is composed of five sections corresponding to the phases of the church service, each of which in turn marks a stage in the drama of Ellen, Grimes, and the child.

(1) Hymn : *Maestoso*, E flat.—Ellen's remarks to the silent child ring the changes on a set of chime-like phrases (doubled by harp and accompanied by chords for lower strings) and are answered by the chorus (off) in rich harmony. The hymn describes a steep dynamic curve and reaches its end just before Ellen discovers the tear in the boy's coat.

(2) Responses : *Recitativo agitato.*—While the organ holds B *ppp.* and the strings sustain a shake on the same note, Ellen makes the discovery that Grimes has been maltreating the child. The tonal centre here and in the following section oscillates between B major and C minor, this enharmonic relationship emerging in full force at the outbreak of :

(3) Gloria : *Andante con moto,* where the words of the chorus are answered by Ellen in a passage which is given an *aria*-like development :

Example 10

(4) Benedicite : *Allegro agitato.*—The onset of this choral unison coincides with the entry of Grimes :

Example 11

The dialogue of Ellen and Grimes is fitted into this framework, with no other accompaniment than an occasional staccato chord from the orchestra to point an accent, until, on Grimes's declaration : " Leave him alone, he's mine ! " a downward passage in triplets, following Ellen's reiterated " Hush, Peter ! " brings the movement to a brief *fermata.* A further short piece of dialogue in *arioso* style ushers in the final section of the *scena* :

(5) Credo: *Adagio.*—The chorus leads off, *ff.*, in unison on F, but are almost immediately " cross-faded " with the horns on the same note, for the entry of Ellen's voice. This horn octave, reiterated in constantly varying note-values, is combined with a theme, marked *espressivo*, to form the basis of a passionate duet, which releases the climax of the scene :

One other phrase in this duet calls for quotation :

When Grimes, giving back despair for despair, strikes Ellen, the music breaks up into a stave of agitated gestures, and the chorus re-enters with an "Amen !" (still on an open F), followed by Grimes's parting cry : " And God have mercy upon me ! "

The lively trio which follows (Auntie, Keene, and Boles) is

4

constructed from this phrase, which remains of capital import-
ance throughout the rest of the act.   As the trio ends the organ
announces the conclusion of the service by a square harmoniza-
tion of Ex. 14, *fff.* ; and Mrs. Sedley and Balstrode arrive on
the scene, the one to assist in working up the general feeling
against Grimes, the other to attempt to quell it.   The chorus
and the rest of the cast are by now assembled on the stage.
From this point until Hobson's drum brings matters to a head,
the musical ensemble falls into four parts, each climax engender-
ing a new section.   In the first, Ex. 14 is transformed into a six-
eight accompaniment figure in C major for the violas and
cellos, interrupted at regular intervals by dominant seventh
chords for the brass which contradict the prevailing tonic.
While half the chorus asks : " What is it ? " the other half
replies : " Grimes is at his exercise."   This vicious scherzo
concludes with a mounting series of the dominant seventh
contradictions mentioned above—a series which serves to land
us in a new key (D major) and a different rhythm (four-four).
In this section Boles plays a predominant part, his shrill tenor
doubled by soft trombone octaves, while the chorus replies
with : " Whoever's guilty gets the rap ! " to an inversion of
Ex. 14.   Auntie's kind entreaty to Ellen lessens the fury of the
music for a few bars, but the movement remains unaltered until
Boles, backed up by the chorus, adjures Ellen to " speak out in
the name of the Lord ! "   This disintegrates the fierce rhythm
and eventually creates a pause ; then Ellen answers with a new
phrase (*andante*) which, together with Mrs. Sedley's comment
on it, provides the material for the third section of this scene.

Example 15

After being developed through several keys, in the course of
which ten solo voices (four female, six male) gradually enter
the harmony, the chorus joins the ensemble in a full statement

of Ex. 15 (this time in A major), in which the three phrases appear in vertical combination, with very full orchestral support. A brilliant cadence is reached without any contrapuntal treatment of the material, and a riotous *stretta* ensues, founded entirely on the following figure :

Example 16

above which the singers insert exclamatory phrases in imitation. At the words : " To Grimes's hut ! "—uttered in unison—the orchestra gallops up to F sharp, then leaves the field clear to a timpani roll and the irregular tap of Hobson's drum (tenor drum). This is worked up into a regular rhythm (*grave*), which is adhered to by the chorus—in unison now for their indignant resolve. This stark and ferocious passage dies down as the procession of villagers recedes into the distance, leaving Ellen, Auntie, and the nieces alone on the stage.

The scene concludes with a quiet, meditative trio (the nieces sing throughout in unison) in purely lyrical style (*andante tranquillo*). There are three verses, each of which has a refrain : " Do we smile or do we weep, Or wait quietly till they sleep ? " The verses are introduced by a downward scale of diatonic seconds for the flutes, like a stream trickling into a calm sea— here described by a rocking figure for muted strings which accompanies the voices. The melody is laid out so as to take advantage of the variable rhythm which results from the three-four against six-eight combination ; but although a certain crescendo of feeling is involved, the song is essentially a static episode, meant to tranquillize our ears and feelings in preparation for a further and more taxing ordeal.

The last of the trickling scales, referred to above, is extended from top to bottom of the register, and serves in this case to bring down the curtain. Started as usual by flutes, it is handed over first to clarinets and then to horns, while the passage is so arranged as to lead the tonality out of D flat into F.

The Interlude which follows is the centre-piece of the whole opera. An extensive Passacaglia on the theme of Ex. 14, it is intended to epitomize the tragedy of Grimes's ambivalent personality—his loneliness, aggravated rather than assuaged by the constant presence of a child too young to give him real companionship ; his need to give, as well as to receive, affection ; and the rudimentary poetic feeling which, while it attaches him entirely to the sea, puts him at odds with the community in which he is obliged to live. At the same time it would not do to shirk the fact that Grimes is guilty of manslaughter : his wilful and choleric nature contains an uncontrollable vein of real ferocity which he is apt to visit on anybody in his power, and especially on the helpless little creatures who, in his better moods, excite in him compassion and tenderness.

Such, then, is the tragic character which lies at the source of this dramatic Interlude. Interwoven with the development of the Passacaglia, the theme of which represents the obdurate will of Grimes himself, is a desolate, wandering motif depicting the workhouse boy who, accustomed no doubt to a steady lack of kindness, does not know how to deal with Grimes's sudden changes of mood and so—as children often do—takes refuge in silence. This theme (in which Grimes sees, not only the solitary boy beside him, but also the innocent child out of which he himself has grown) is heard first as a viola solo, accompanied only by the Passacaglia theme, *pizzicato*, with brief timpani rolls :

Example 17ª
Andante moderato

As the theme winds upwards and out of sight, like a thread of smoke, the first variation starts, in a brisker measure, with the theme in sharp diminution :

Example 17b
animando

This is developed to a considerable orchestral climax, then reduced to the persistent ground bass, above which Ex. 17 (*a*) recurs—harmonized, this time, in a very tense manner. Half-way through its development it acquires a rhythmically regular accompaniment of open fourths. At the end of the development the brass builds up, hand over hand, then dismantles and builds up anew in slightly altered form, a series of chords based on Ex. 17 (*a*). These disappear, as usual, back into the Passacaglia, and a syncopated version of Ex. 17 (*a*), marked *agitato* and scored for muted horns and strings played *col legno*, leads to a strange, pathetic sequence for the upper strings in imitation :

Example 17ᶜ

From this point until the rise of the curtain the music builds a long *crescendo*, and although the regular beat of the Passacaglia preserves the original tempo, an effect of increasing movement and agitation is obtained by gradually diminishing the note-values in the middle and upper parts. The thematic material remains the same, but in this fourth and final variation the harmony becomes still more angular and intense. Trumpets and wood-wind join the strings in a rushing climax, which brings up the curtain on Grimes's singular dwelling—an upturned boat on the cliff's edge, its dark and squalid interior crowded with nets, rope, and tackle of all kinds.

Scene 2

From the rise of the curtain to the entry of the villagers, after the boy's death, this scene consists entirely of a monologue for Grimes : the only sound uttered by the child is his scream as he falls down the cliff.

The stormy climax of the Interlude, on which the curtain rises, leads straight into an angry cadenza, sung to the words " Go there ! " by Grimes as he enters the hut, thrusting the boy in front of him. Savage fragments of Ex. 17 (*a*) punctuate the recitative, but give way to a version of Ex. 17 (*c*), transformed

with a curious, remote tenderness as Grimes catches sight of the
jersey Ellen knitted for him.   This breaks off as Grimes's ill-
temper returns, and the boy's theme is flung violently about in
cadenza-like fashion, by brass and violins.   The music calms
down once more, as Grimes seeks to distract the boy from the
fright he has caused him.   But the sight of the boiling sea,
through the cliff door, reminds him that fish must be caught and
money made, to stop the mouths of the " Borough gossips," and
he launches into a tirade against the latter reminiscent of a
kindred passage in Act I (see p. 35).   " I'll marry . . ." he concludes, musingly, as the scherzando dies down—then, catching
sight of the boy still sitting on a coil of rope, he bids him roughly
take off his shirt, put on his jersey, and prepare to go to sea.
The music here again draws on Ex. 17 (a) for a series of sinister
progressions, underpinned by a deep, repeated F sharp for the
double basses, and followed by a hasty outburst of Ex. 17 (b) for
flutes and brass, which sinks down, through a string passage
founded on the same theme, to a more lyrical form of recitative.
Grimes now tries to pacify the boy by painting a picture of life
as it might be, if only circumstances and his own character
were more harmonious.   The air which develops out of this
passage is of an idyllic character and the voice part highly florid.
The accompaniment figure :

Example 18
Adagio

is given first to the wood-wind and later (in a fuller harmoniza-
tion) to muted violins.   At the end of the air the foregoing
recitative returns, this time in a more agitated form, and a
winding passage for the strings builds a mysterious chord :

Example 19

against which Hobson's drum is heard approaching, *ppp*. As Grimes continues his meditation, the drum stops and Ex. 18 is heard in distorted form and in the higher wood-wind. These two sequences alternate until Hobson's drum, and the chorus which is following it, become audible to Grimes. This gives instant rise to a neurotic outburst of rage and suspicion, directed against the boy. The material here repeats the third variation of the Passacaglia (staccato syncopation with *col legno* strings), while Hobson's drum-taps grow inexorably nearer and in ever closer rhythmical formation. The chorus, chanting their rigid little tune (heard at the end of Scene 1), is by now quite loud. As Grimes shouts accusingly at the boy, the Passacaglia theme returns in its inverted form, scored for low wood-wind and harp, while muted trumpets repeat an octave figure, *pp.*, off the beat.

Grimes commands the boy to go out and climb down the cliff-face to the shore. As he hesitates, the chorus come nearer and nearer, still singing their tune in unison to the words : " Bring the branding iron and knife, What's done now is done for life." Then, while the basses, trombones, and timpani keep up an agitated figure composed of the Passacaglia theme inverted, a series of tumultuous upward scale passages, for violas and cellos in octaves, bring the boy to the cliff door. As he starts to climb out, the crowd is heard knocking at the door on the opposite side of the hut, and the whole orchestra, starting with oboes, clarinets and cymbals, perform a high shake on B, A sharp, C. Strings add themselves, then muted brass. As the boy loses his foothold and falls down the cliff-side, the orchestral din ceases abruptly, leaving the lonely scream of terror echoing on and on in the unearthly tones of the celesta, as Grimes himself climbs down the cliff :

Example 20

These arpeggios continue *ad lib.* through the ensuing dialogue, until Swallow creates a diversion with a sententious speech : " The whole affair gives Boro' talk its—shall I say quietus." This comic little interlude, intentionally quite out of keeping with the rest of the picture, is a jaunty little tune in B flat,

accompanied only by bassoon and tuba, and strongly reminiscent
of the musical setting of the Prologue (Ex. 1 is even quoted).
The coda accompanies the crestfallen villagers out of the hut,
leaving Balstrode, who alone suspects that all is not well.   As
he stands looking round, the echo of the scream returns in the
murmuring arpeggios of the celesta, and the ghost of the dead
boy wails faintly in a long, wandering passage for solo viola,
similar to that of Ex. 17 (*a*).   Balstrode sees the child's Sunday
clothes, examines them, goes to the cliff door and leans right out
—then, as the celesta music sinks further and further towards
middle C, he climbs down the cliff after Grimes and the boy.
The theme of the Passacaglia is heard once more, *ppp.*, from the
cellos and basses, *pizzicato*, as the curtain falls.

ACT III

The orchestral prelude with which this act opens is somewhat
larger in scope, and a good deal profounder in feeling, than
those which introduce Acts I and II.   The scene it sets is that
of the town and harbour lying tranquil under a moonlit sky ;
but there are no pictorial effects in the orchestral writing :   the
music is spare and homogeneous, the imaginative effect that of
a mood, simple yet intense :

Example 21ᵃ
Andante con moto e rubato

Example 21ᵇ

As may perhaps not be obvious from the appearance of
Ex. 21 (*a*), this strings-and-horns texture is essentially contrapuntal—not a sequence of chords ;   throughout this prelude
there are really only four voices and they climb slowly into the

higher registers through a chain of keys (C, B minor, D flat) that lands us back in the original key and the original position without the addition of any extraneous material. The little phrases for flute-and-harp (Ex. 21 (*b*)) may be regarded as a form of punctuation to mark the paragraphs in what might otherwise seem an obscurely continuous movement ; but they also illumine and decorate the whole, as the moonlight illumines the town. The first chord of Ex. 21 (*a*) is worth remarking ; its isolation has for object the establishing of that inversion of the common chord upon which each subsequent instance of the sequence is founded. As the final statements of the theme disintegrate, leaving the harp and flute to glint sharply in the silence, the curtain rises on :

Scene 1

The music of this scene, with the exception of a single *aria*, is elaborated from the four dances which proceed, with short interruptions, from the Moot Hall. All through the scene the band on the stage either alternates with the orchestra or is dovetailed with it, and in the first section (a barn dance), the flute continues for a page to repeat its little figure from the prelude, and by holding the final note subtly influences the foursquare harmony of the dance :

Example 22

The first voice to enter is that of Swallow ; he sings a beery, sprawling tune, with great lunges of a tenth (B flat to D flat), against the lilting triplets of the band. The nieces join in, picking their notes with less abandon, and eventually all three are singing together, the nieces in canon, Swallow plodding along (here the band is in B flat, against the E flat of the orchestra and singers). The barn dance ends with a percussion solo from

the band, capped immediately, as Swallow goes disgustedly
into The Boar, by a fortissimo statement of his tune from the
orchestra.   Ned Keene now supervenes, and during his play
with the nieces the striding theme is treated canonically, so as
to lower the musical temperature and modulate into C major
for the next dance, which is a waltz of the *Ländler* type with an
oddly Lisztian flavour :

Example 23

This gives the cue for the entry of Mrs. Sedley, who is seen
in this act in what the librettist conceives to be a malignant
light—*i.e.* determined that Grimes shall receive summary
justice for the murder of the little boy.   As the waltz proceeds
Mrs. Sedley, in measured recitative, makes Keene free of her
discovery, and as Keene abuses her for scandal-mongering the
band introduces a new theme :

Example 24

The orchestra re-enters for Mrs. Sedley's words : " Murder
most foul it is.   Eerie I find it," and cellos double her part :

Example 25

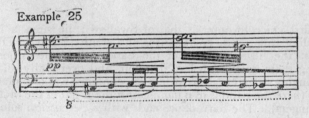

Ex. 23 and 24 return once more in combination, then the scene is brought to an end by a transition passage constructed from Ex. 25, which modulates into the key of A flat for the next dance —a hornpipe. This breaks from the band as the Rector and others come upon the stage:

Example 26

In the ensuing short scene the Rector's solo alternates with a male chorus singing in unison, against the constant background of the hornpipe, in which the orchestra makes a few interjections. The company disperses, singing " Good-night," and the hornpipe rhythm fades imperceptibly into a return of Ex. 25, as the interest shifts back to Mrs. Sedley. Her words are accompanied by the basses, a solo cello, and a muted trumpet, in canonic imitation, while the middle part is filled by the violins and violas.

This leads, through a page of recitative for Ellen and Balstrode, to an *aria* for the former, as she contemplates the boy's jersey which she has found, with its broidered anchor on the chest. " Embroidery in childhood was a luxury of idleness," she muses.

Example 27

Hitherto each section of the scene has carried the action a
step forward, but here in this brief *aria*—as in the trio at the end
of Act II, Scene 1—the tragedy halts for a moment before
hurrying on to (in this case final) catastrophe.   The *aria* has
two verses, and the voice part, of which the *tessitura* is in the
main high, is extremely florid ; but the whole effect is tranquil
and flowing.   The accompaniment preserves the form taken in
Ex. 27, except during the refrain : " Now my broidery affords
the clue whose meaning we avoid," where the halting fall of
the voice is accompanied by organ chords, *ppp.*, and flute
octaves in imitation of the voice.

With the end of the *aria* the strings and *cor anglais* pick up
the pattern of the preceding recitative, which is then developed
into a passage of *arioso* for Balstrode : " When horror breaks
one heart, all hearts are broken."   The scene ends with a return
of Ex. 14, sung in counterpoint to the words " We shall be there
with him," in its original position by Balstrode and in inversion
by Ellen, sustained by a chord of B major for the four horns.

As Ellen and Balstrode leave the stage the band in the Moot
Hall strikes up a Galop (*allegro molto*) which has two themes :

Example 28ᵃ

and :

Example 28ᵇ

These themes, combined later with Ex. 25, assist Mrs. Sedley to work up the dance into a man-hunt for Grimes. Major and minor seconds are an important ingredient of the vocal writing in this section, conferring on the whole scene an atmosphere of hysterical tension and brutality. In the first section Mrs. Sedley, Hobson, Swallow, and Auntie are accompanied in their staccato counterpoint by the band alone ; but as, in answer to Hobson's call : " Come out and help ! Grimes is around ! " the people begin to stream out of the Moot Hall, the band is cross-faded with the orchestra in a deep statement of Ex. 25, which is developed in combination with a subsidiary idea :

Example 29

Six soloists (the nieces, Mrs. Sedley, Boles, Keene, and Swallow), singing as a quartet, now divide themselves from the main body of the singers, and the two groups hand Ex. 28 (*b*) backwards and forwards, modulating in semitones as they do so, until, at the words : " Him who despises us we'll destroy ! " Ex. 29 returns, in increasingly close canon, for both chorus and soloists. This *stretta* emerges into a tumultuous statement of Ex. 28 (*a*) for brass, and thence into a return—for full orchestra and all the singers—of Ex. 24. As the people begin to disperse in all directions, to look for Grimes, the dance-fabric breaks up into isolated gestures for the voices calling " Peter Grimes ! " while the orchestra performs an agitated semiquaver figure. This leads swiftly to three hammer blows, *tutti*, followed by a series of descending fifths which diminish steeply in volume with the fall of the curtain.

The interlude, which is brief, is one of the strangest and most imaginative passages in the opera. A thick fog creeps in from the sea and swathes the town ; in the fuliginous blackness which matches that of his own soul Grimes, weary in body and half-demented, makes his way back to the harbour and his boat— the only refuge he has left from the torment of his guilt. The music, which transfers us from he one-track hysteria of the

crowd to the echoing limbo of Grimes's mind, is an orchestral
cadenza the disrupted elements of which are bound together
by a single chord—a dominant seventh on D—held, *ppp.*, throughout the interlude by three muted horns. Figures of nightmare,
sea-birds fly through the fog uttering fragments of themes
which Grimes has sung earlier in the opera—first the gossip
theme of Act I (solo flute), then, after a reminiscence of the
voice part of Ex. 18, played very softly by the harp in its lowest
octaves, a version of Ex. 5 from three solo violins at the opposite
end of the register. This is interrupted by a mocking fragment
of Ex. 6, again for the flute, answered by Ex. 5, this time from
the basses and double bassoon, below a grunting figure for two
clarinets. This in turn vanishes into the iridescent dominant
seventh chord, which is always uncovered, like a watery moon,
whenever the nightmare cries fall silent. Finally a big climax,
covering the whole compass, is built up, and at the top of it the
theme of the Passacaglia (Ex. 14) is enunciated, *fff.*, in a passage
which comprehends both the inverted and the original forms of
the theme. But Grimes's will, though violent, has no staying
power, and so the theme which expresses it falters at once—
falters and breaks down, leaving the immitigable horn chord
where it has always been, as it were a force of Nature. When
the curtain rises on the final scene, the distant chorus takes over
the chord, *pp.*, while below it the fog-horn (a tuba off-stage)
begins to sound.

Scene 2

Until the death of Grimes, and the gradual break of day, the
music consists of a recitative for Grimes himself, and later for
Ellen, accompanied only by (1) the calling of the townspeople
—now distant, now near at hand—as they pursue their sinister
game of hide-and-seek, and (2) the lowing of the fog-horn.

Example 30

As in the foregoing interlude, but now to a much fuller

extent, the broken phrases sung by Grimes in his desperate state recall every stage of his tragic story : sometimes the voices of the chorus calling his name interrupt his speech, at others, assisted by the tuba, they provide quite a fully harmonized accompaniment to it. Each section of the recitative is so designed as to end on E flat, which is taken up by the tuba at degrees of loudness which vary with the quality of Grimes's emotion and the proximity of the crowd. But when at last all his thoughts forsake him and he is at his lowest ebb, the cries die away entirely and for the last time the fog-horn winds its desolate, inhuman throat. Then Balstrode, who has been waiting with Ellen, comes up to Grimes, and in a short passage of spoken dialogue tells him what he must do.

When Grimes has pushed off from shore in his boat to sink and drown, life begins to return with the dawn and its infinitesimal announcement by three solo violins. Slowly, very gradually, the music with which Act I opened returns to the orchestra (Ex. 2), gathering in strength and volume and definition as the light dispels the mist and begins to outline the houses, the lighthouse, and the townspeople who start about their ordinary business. It is just "the cold beginning of another day"; the tragedy is forgotten. The chorus begin to sing and their song is the same as before (in Act I), while the strings draw and re-draw their chord and the water slaps against the boats and trickles over the stones of the harbour in the little harp-and-clarinet arpeggios. As before, the tonality combines both A major and A minor, the former eventually predominating as the chorus, singing in unison, swells in volume. Swallow sees a boat sinking, far out at sea, and calls the attention of one of the fishermen to it. But nothing is done : the movement of the music remains quite undisturbed, and as those who have played their part in the tragedy are drawn back once more into the general life of the township, the sturdy diatonic setting of Crabbe's words reaches its climax and then is reabsorbed by the orchestral *ostinato*. This too disintegrates as the curtain falls, and the opera ends, *ppp.*, with the following chord, scored for strings and trombones :

Example 31